WHY MUM?

WHY MUM?

A Small Child Dealing with a Big Problem

BY CATHERINE THORNTON

Illustrations by Robert Thornton

To

Paul,

Robert, Simon

and especially

Matthew

who inspired this book.

Thanks a million guys.

INTRODUCTION

This book is about me and my family, especially my youngest son Matthew.

It was written because I got very sick about five years ago and it was very hard on the whole family. I felt that it was particularly hard on Matthew as he was only seven and he and I had spent a lot of time together. We had fun and my being sick changed a lot of the things I could do with him.

This made him sad and mixed-up and even a little angry. He couldn't understand what was happening and why it was happening and I found it hard to explain to him. I looked in the bookshops to try to find a book that might help us talk about what was going on but I couldn't find one.

When I got better I decided to try and write one myself. Matthew thought it was a good idea to do this and said that the book might help other girls and boys like him. I hope this book will also help parents. We have lived through what we thought was a very bad time for our family, but it did come to an end and I did get better, with the help of doctors and medicine, and also with the help of family and friends who showed their love in so many ways.

Matthew and I would like to share our times in that difficult year and maybe you will read something in here that will help you. Maybe you will even enjoy the book; it's not about being sad or miserable, it's about a family dealing with tough times together.

My name is Matthew and I'm eight. I live with my Mum
and Dad and my two big brothers (and I really mean big –
they are grown-up people like Mum and Dad). My Mum
doesn't go out to work like some of my friends' mothers;
she stays home and minds me.

She collects me from school each day and we have races home. I usually win;
I think she lets me sometimes. I tell her she doesn't have to do this because I'm
not a baby anymore and I won't cry if I lose. She crossed her heart and said I
was really winning now that I'm getting so tall and my legs are so long she can't
catch up on me anymore. She says I will soon be taller than her and then she
will have to look up at everybody in the house!

We often go to the park after school and I love going to the playground and riding my bike. My Mum is older than some of my friends' Mums because my two brothers were big when I was born. Simon is ten years older than me and is allowed to do lots of things I can't. It's like having three Dads sometimes when they all start telling me what to do, but I have fun with them too and sometimes they take me out when Mum and Dad can't. They can help me with my homework as well.

Robert can drive the car and takes me to the pictures and that's really cool and it makes my friends jealous when I tell them. Simon helps me to practise my hurling so I will be good enough for the school team.

One day when I was only seven, a long time ago, I was in the sitting room sorting through my Pokémon cards, trying to decide which ones I wanted to trade with my friend Stephen when I heard what sounded like my mum crying in the kitchen.

This scared me because I had never heard her crying like that before except over some stupid kissing film on the TV. I went and peeped into the kitchen and there she was sitting with a cup of coffee in one hand and a soggy, messy-looking tissue in the other.

I didn't know what to do.

I wanted to run back to my cards and pretend that I hadn't heard anything, but I didn't want to leave her on her own either. Where are big brothers when you really need them?

She never even heard me come in and she jumped when I put my hand on her shoulder. I wasn't sure what to say, but I wanted to know what was wrong. I was afraid that something had happened to Dad or my brothers and I was afraid to ask.

She put her arm around me and squeezed me tight. Now I like hugs from my Mum when I know none of my friends are watching, but this one was going on a long time.

Then she let me go and looked at me kind of funny.

'I'm sorry if I frightened you, Matthew. I want to talk to you for a minute, I have something I want to tell you,' she said.

Good call

I didn't like this as it sounded kind of serious, but I sat down on a kitchen stool beside her. She didn't say anything for a few minutes; she just looked as if she was trying to stop crying again.

'I have to go into hospital for seven or eight days,' she said. 'I'm sick and the doctors want to do an operation that will help me get better. Dad and your brothers will mind you when I'm not here and you can come and see me in the hospital every day.'

I didn't say anything because I didn't really understand what she meant, so I just said 'OK' and ran back to play with my cards. I felt all funny inside. I heard Dad come in and Mum talking to him in the kitchen. He came into me in the sitting room and asked if he could have a chat with me for a minute.

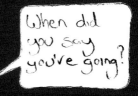

When did you say you've going?

'Mum is sorry that you heard her crying,' he said. 'She asked me if I would explain to you what's going on.' He took me onto his knee and I snuggled into him and felt safe.

'Your mum has a thing called cancer,' Dad told me 'and the doctors have said that she has to have an operation and some medicine to make it better.'

'They want her to go into hospital in a few days and she'll be staying there for a little while until she's strong enough to come home. Then I'll need you and Robert and Simon to help me until she is OK again,' he said.

'What's cancer?' I asked. 'Does it hurt?'

'Mum's not sore at all now,' said Dad. 'That's why they want to do the operation quickly. Cancer is sick cells in the body that shouldn't be there and they have to be taken out. She will be sore afterwards but we won't worry about that for the moment. Why don't you go in and give her a big hug?'

Bad cell

After that day a lot of
things changed at home. Mum went
into hospital and instead of her collecting
me from school, I had to go to my friend Andrew's
house; his Mum minded me until Dad got home from work.

It was fun going to his house and playing with him, but it wasn't the same as being with my Mum. His Mum wanted to give me my lunch, but she cooked different things than my Mum did and I had none of my toys to play with. I had to watch whatever the others were watching on the television. It didn't feel right.

When Dad collected me we had to hurry home and get dinner quickly so that he could go and see Mum in the hospital.

GET WELL SOON MUM!

He brought me in to see her the first Sunday after she had gone in. The hospital smelled funny, like the bathroom after Mum has used her cleaning stuff, and she was in a room with other women all in their nightclothes. I wasn't sure what to say, but I gave her the card I had made for her. She had a funny bottle on the ground beside her that had a tube in it out of her side. 'That's all the bad stuff draining out and when it is finished I will be coming home,' she told me. I cried that night when I went to bed because the hospital seemed very far away and I wanted my Mum to read me my bedtime story.

WELCOME HOME MUM!

When Mum came home she walked very slowly and Dad had to help her to sit on the couch. I went to give her a hug and Dad grabbed me quickly.

'You can't hug Mum at the moment,' he said. 'She feels too sore right now. You need to be careful for a while.'

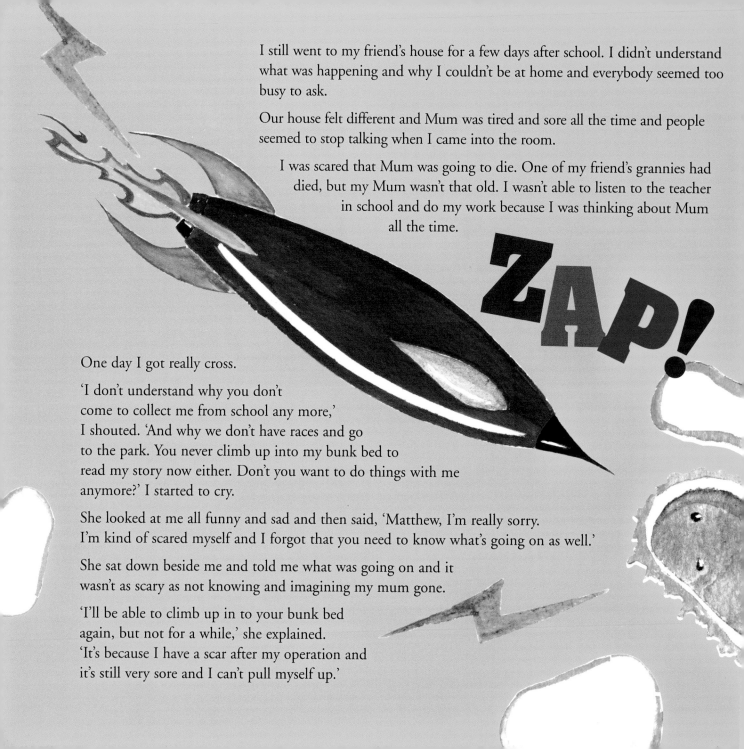

I still went to my friend's house for a few days after school. I didn't understand what was happening and why I couldn't be at home and everybody seemed too busy to ask.

Our house felt different and Mum was tired and sore all the time and people seemed to stop talking when I came into the room.

I was scared that Mum was going to die. One of my friend's grannies had died, but my Mum wasn't that old. I wasn't able to listen to the teacher in school and do my work because I was thinking about Mum all the time.

ZAP!

One day I got really cross.

'I don't understand why you don't come to collect me from school any more,' I shouted. 'And why we don't have races and go to the park. You never climb up into my bunk bed to read my story now either. Don't you want to do things with me anymore?' I started to cry.

She looked at me all funny and sad and then said, 'Matthew, I'm really sorry. I'm kind of scared myself and I forgot that you need to know what's going on as well.'

She sat down beside me and told me what was going on and it wasn't as scary as not knowing and imagining my mum gone.

'I'll be able to climb up in to your bunk bed again, but not for a while,' she explained. 'It's because I have a scar after my operation and it's still very sore and I can't pull myself up.'

'The operation has taken away all the cancer that the doctors could see,' she went on. 'But now I need to have some special medicine in case any of it is hiding. I'll have to go to the hospital for one day every three weeks to get this medicine.'

The medicine, which had a funny big name – 'chemotherapy' (I had to get her to spell it for me) – would make her a bit sick. It didn't know the difference between the good cells and the bad cells and would zap them both. The good cells would grow back, but it would take a while.

Good cell

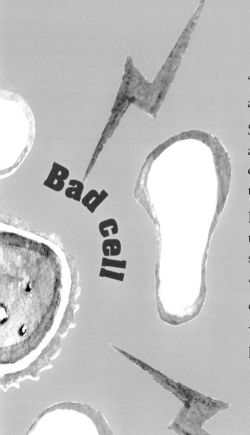

Bad cell

'Matthew, I know this is a lot for you to understand. I'm just learning about it all myself,' Mum said.

She promised to talk to me and tell me what was happening as it went along and that I could ask her any questions I wanted to. 'We'll find other ways to have fun together,' she promised. 'And you can snuggle up to me in my bed and I'll read you a story there.'

I felt a bit better after this, but Mum said that taking the medicine would go on for nine months and that seemed like ages.

'I'll be finished shortly after you move into second class,' said Mum.

We were only at my birthday now; the Easter holidays hadn't even come yet.

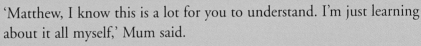

HAPPY BIRTHDAY MATTHEW

Mum got her first medicine – it's called treatment – on the Friday before my birthday party. I was afraid that my party wouldn't happen but she promised that Dad would take me and my friends to the adventure centre even if she couldn't go. But she was OK and came along. Maybe it wasn't going to be too bad after all.

After a couple of her treatments Mum started to feel tired and she needed to go for a nap sometimes. Andrew's mum used to bring me home from school and I knew, when I came in, that sometimes Mum was just out of bed.

She had talked to my teacher and told her what was happening so that I didn't get into trouble if my homework wasn't done or I felt funny in class sometimes.

I just wanted things to be back the way they were. I know it wasn't Mum's fault that she was sick, but sometimes I still felt cross at her because she couldn't do things. It was a mixed-up sort of feeling and I didn't like it.

Some days Mum was feeling well and we nearly forgot she was sick.

The treatment made all her hair fall out and she had to wear a wig. When she wasn't wearing it she kept it on a glass head in her bedroom and it looked weird. She used to get upset if anybody came to the door and she hadn't got it on so I used to run and get it for her if she needed it in a hurry. It was kind of cool running down the stairs and spinning it on my fingers.

Some days my Mum used to laugh about her bald head but I saw her on windy days holding on tight to the wig as if she was afraid it would blow away.

Around the time I got my summer holidays Mum had to go for another treatment called radiotherapy. She had to go to a different hospital for this and I went with her a couple of mornings.

It was good fun there. They had a play area where I could play when Mum was getting her treatment. She had to lie on a bed and not move for a few minutes. She told me it was like having an X-ray. Sometimes the nurses would talk to me and show me how the machines worked.

She had to go there every day for a good while so sometimes I stayed with Robert or Simon or sometimes at my friend's house. When she came home we would go somewhere if she was able.

I loved going out to Bray to the **aquarium** and seeing all the **fish**, they even had small **sharks** there, and we would go for **burger and chips afterwards as well.**

One day a few weeks after the summer holidays Mum told me that her last treatment was the next day. 'Does this mean that you're fine again?' I asked hopefully.

She said the doctors would have to check her and that she would still be tired for a while, but that all the bad cancer cells had gone away.

It was nearly a year from when Dad first told me that Mum was sick and I was eight now instead of seven.

Mum told me that I had been such a help to her when she was sick.

'Thank you for being such a great boy and helping Dad so much. I don't know what we would have done without you,' she said and gave me a big squashy hug just like she used to before all this being sick started.

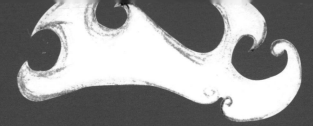

It's nearly summer again now and my Mum climbs up on my bunk to read my story again. We even had a race the other day.

I came in the other day and Mum and Dad and my brothers were whispering about something and suddenly stopped. I felt my tummy go all funny and I must have looked scared because Mum jumped up and ran over to me.

'There's nothing wrong Matthew,' she said quickly. 'We're just making plans for a special holiday for all the family this year, since we didn't have any last year. We were going to keep it as a surprise, but it's even better if we can all plan it together.'

So we're all off to France and I get to fly in an aeroplane for the first time. It's great to have Mum back doing all sorts of things with me.

. . . up, up and away

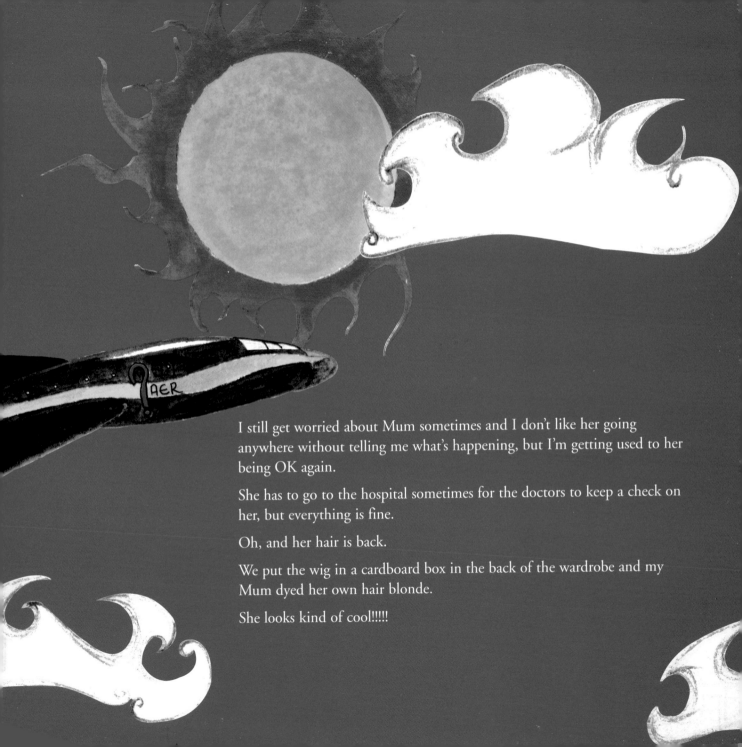

I still get worried about Mum sometimes and I don't like her going anywhere without telling me what's happening, but I'm getting used to her being OK again.

She has to go to the hospital sometimes for the doctors to keep a check on her, but everything is fine.

Oh, and her hair is back.

We put the wig in a cardboard box in the back of the wardrobe and my Mum dyed her own hair blonde.

She looks kind of cool!!!!!